SAFETY FIRST

On the
Road

Ruth Thomson

Commissioned photography by
Chris Fairclough

W

FRANKLIN WATTS
LONDON • SYDNEY

© 2004 Franklin Watts

First published in 2004 by
Franklin Watts
96 Leonard Street
London
EC2A 4XD

Franklin Watts Australia
45-51 Huntley Street
Alexandria
NSW 2015

ISBN: 0 7496 5467 8

Printed in Malaysia
Planning and production by Discovery Books Limited
Editor: Helena Attlee
Designer: Ian Winton
Consultants: Alison Curtis, Manager Streetwise Safety Centre
and Nevil Tillman, Bournemouth Road Safety Centre.

The author, packager and publisher would like to thank the following people for their
participation in this book: Juliana, Adam and Ieuan Crowe; Jane, Lauren and Katie Neal;
Parveen, Abdullah, Sara and Aisha Iqbal.

Contents

A safe route to school

It is a sunny day, and Adam wants to walk to school instead of going by car.

Adam leaves home in good time with his Mum and Ieuan, his younger brother. They remember to walk inside the kerb. 'Let's hold hands,' says Ieuan, 'so we can keep each other safe.'

Driveways and exits

The boys are so busy talking that they don't notice a car suddenly backing out of a driveway in front of them. Adam shouts and jumps back.
'You must watch out for danger on the pavement as well as on the road,' Mum tells them.

SAFETY FACTS

Use all your senses to avoid cars coming out of driveways. You will:
• See the reversing lights.
• Smell the exhaust.
• Hear the engine.

The Green Cross Code

Mum asks Adam to show Ieuan how to use the Green Cross Code to cross the quiet road where they live.

Think

Adam chooses the safest place to cross. He can see clearly both ways along the road. There are no parked cars to block his view, and no bends or junctions.

Stop

They wait on the pavement, a little way back from the kerb.

Look and listen

They all look in both directions, checking for traffic.
'I can see a car coming,' says Ieuan.

Wait until it is safe to cross

They wait for the car to pass. Then they look around and listen once more.

Walk, don't run

When the road is completely clear, they cross.
'Never run across a road, in case you fall over,' Adam reminds Ieuan, 'and always walk straight across, not diagonally.'

Arrive alive

'Well done,' says Mum. 'Don't forget to use the Green Cross Code every time you cross a road.'

A zebra crossing

At the end of their road, they come to a busier street. Adam chooses a safe place to cross – a zebra crossing.

They stand at the kerb, waiting for the traffic to stop. Mum says, 'Try to catch a driver's eye, so you know he has seen you waiting.'

SAFETY FACTS

- Always cross on the black and white stripes of a zebra crossing.
- Never cross on the zig-zag lines on either side of it as this can be dangerous.

Crossing safely

They wait until the traffic stops in both directions. 'Keep looking and listening,' Adam tells Ieuan as they cross, 'in case there's a driver who hasn't seen us.'

Traffic islands

- Some roads have a traffic island in the middle.
- Use the Green Cross Code to cross to the middle.
- Wait between the bollards until the other side of the road is clear.
- Use the Green Cross Code to cross again.

Main roads

When they reach the main road, the children stop by a safety barrier.

'We need to be especially careful now, because traffic goes much faster along here,' Mum says.

Bus and cycle lanes

Mum points out the bus lane and cycle lane marked on the road. 'Cars and lorries are not allowed to drive or park here,' she says, 'so buses can speed along particularly fast.'

'Cyclists go fast too,' says Adam, as one whizzes down the road.

Subways

They walk along the road to a subway that goes underneath the road. 'This is the safest place to cross a busy road,' says Mum.

Subways are pedestrian tunnels built under main roads. If a road has a subway, this shows that it is a very busy and dangerous road.

Footbridges

Some main roads that are dangerous to cross have footbridges over them. Use the footbridge if you can.

Travelling by bus

Now the children walk past some shops, and a bus stop where a crowd of people are waiting on the pavement.

'Soon, we will be old enough to catch the bus by ourselves,' says Ieuan.
'Yes,' says Mum, 'but you will need to learn which bus to catch or you will go the wrong way.'

SAFETY FACTS

- Do not cross the road close to a parked vehicle or a bus that has stopped, as you might step out in front of a car.
- Wait for the vehicle to move, or find a safer place to cross.

Bus stops

There are signs at the bus stop to tell you which buses stop there. Sometimes there is a timetable that shows you how often the buses run, as well.

SAFETY FACTS

Boarding a bus

- When the bus arrives, wait for the people to get off before you try to get on.
- Wait in the queue to pay your fare.

Traffic lights

The children reach a junction. Traffic lights control the traffic in all directions.

Ieuan watches the lights. 'Have you ever noticed how traffic lights always change in the same order?' he asks.

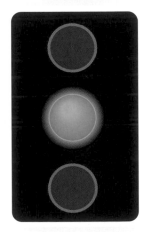

SAFETY FACTS

Traffic lights change in this order.
RED to RED AND AMBER to GREEN.
GREEN to AMBER to RED.

Red	Red and amber	Green	Amber

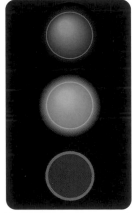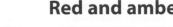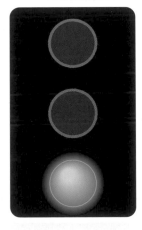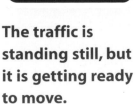

All traffic must stop.

The traffic is standing still, but it is getting ready to move.

Traffic can go if the road ahead is clear.

The lights are changing. Traffic should stop, but cars already on or past the stop line may still be moving.

Red traffic lights

'Be careful!' says Mum. 'Some of the traffic lights are red, but there is a green arrow telling cars that they can turn left.'

'Yes, look!' says Adam, pointing to cars speeding around the corner.

Road signs

As they turn a corner, Adam spots a road sign. 'Look,' he says, 'we are in a one-way street.'

'Well done,' says Mum. She reminds Adam and Ieuan to check which way the traffic is going before they cross the road.

Giving messages

'Let's see how many different kinds of road signs we can spot on our way,' says Mum.

No entry

School crossing ahead

Signs in red triangles give warnings.

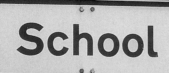

Signs with red circles tell drivers what not to do.

No through road
Rectangular signs give information.

Emergency vehicles

Just then, a fire engine rushes past, its siren screaming. 'Stand still!' says Mum. 'You should freeze if you hear an ambulance, police car or fire engine, or see its lights flashing. Get out of the way if you need to, but otherwise it's best not to move until it has passed.'

Pedestrian crossings

Mum, Adam and Ieuan reach a main road where there is a pelican crossing. Ieuan presses the button that controls the traffic lights and a WAIT signal appears.

There is no traffic, but the man signal is still red. Someone starts to cross the road.

'There's nothing coming; can't we cross now?' Adam asks.

'No,' Mum replies. 'If a car came along the driver might not see you.'

When the green man lights up and the bleeping sound begins, they start crossing. They are only half way across when the green man signal starts flashing.

'Don't worry,' says Mum, 'we've got plenty of time to reach the other side. But remember, never start to cross the road if the green man signal is flashing.'

Puffin crossings

Puffin crossings have a box with a red and green man above the controls.

If the man is red, press the control button. Don't cross until the green man is lit.

When crossing the road, always walk between the two rows of studs.

School crossing patrols

Finally, they reach their school. Some of Adam's and Ieuan's friends are on the other side of the road. They are waiting for the school crossing patrol. The patrolman will tell them when to cross.

A near miss!

Adam spots his friend Alice across the road. Without thinking or looking, he steps into the road.
'Adam, stop!' shouts Ieuan.

Adam steps quickly back on to the pavement.
Mum rushes up to him.

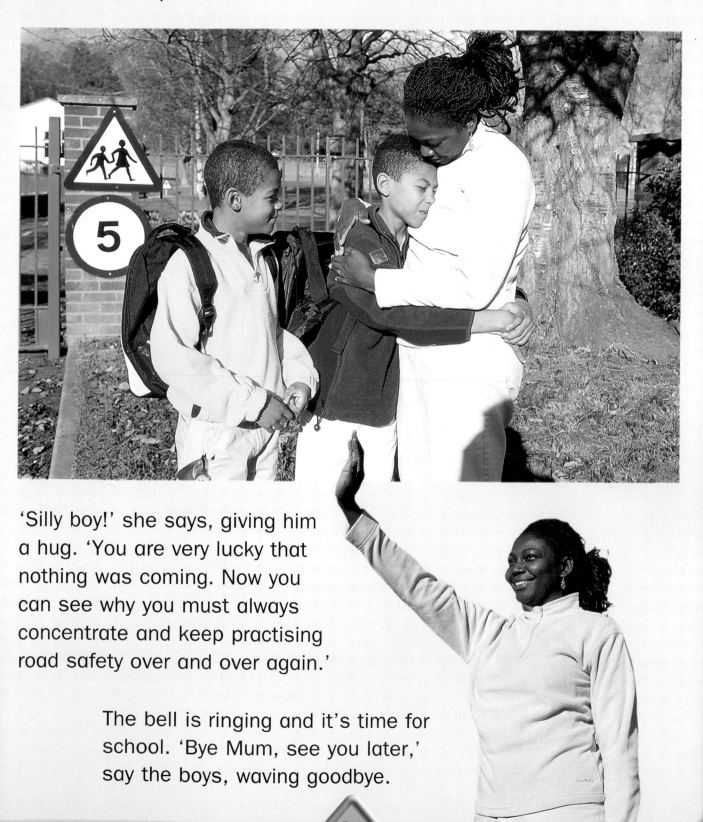

'Silly boy!' she says, giving him
a hug. 'You are very lucky that
nothing was coming. Now you
can see why you must always
concentrate and keep practising
road safety over and over again.'

The bell is ringing and it's time for
school. 'Bye Mum, see you later,'
say the boys, waving goodbye.

Ready for a car journey

Adam is doing a school project about farms. At the weekend he asks Mum if they can go into the country. He needs to look at some cows to try and tell what kind they are.

'I know just the place,' says Mum. 'Let's go by car.' Adam and Ieuan get into the car, using the door on the pavement side.

Car doors

'Watch your fingers now,' says Mum, as she closes the door.
She checks that it is firmly shut and that the child safety locks are on.

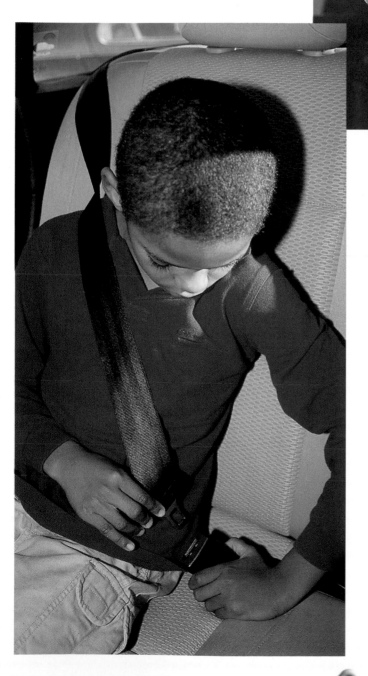

SAFETY FACTS

- Keep your hands away from door handles while the car is moving.
- Wait for a grown-up to open the door for you, once the car has stopped.

Clunk, click, every trip

As soon as they're both inside the car, Adam and Ieuan do up their seatbelts. Mum makes sure that they are both secure. 'Did you know,' says Mum, 'the law says you must always wear a seatbelt in a moving car?'

Travelling by car

Mum has to concentrate when she is driving. The boys sit quietly in the back. They both look at the map to see where they are going.

SAFETY FACTS

The view in the mirror

Do not block the rear-view mirror, otherwise the driver will not be able to see the traffic coming up from behind.

No throwing

Adam winds down his window to throw out the peel from his tangerine, but Mum stops him just in time.

'That could be dangerous,' she says. 'Imagine what might happen if it hit the windscreen of a fast, oncoming car or a motorcyclist! You must never lean out of the window either, or hang anything out of it.'

'That's a funny sign,' says Ieuan. 'It looks like a false moustache!' 'It means that the road ahead is uneven,' laughs Mum. 'Some country road signs are different from those in the town. See what else you can spot.'

Walking on country roads

Mum parks the car off the road, and they set out to look for some cows. There is no pavement here, so they have to walk along the side of the road.

In single file

They walk on the right-hand side of the road, so they can see cars coming towards them, and the drivers can see them, too.

'Keep in single file,' says Mum, 'and listen out for traffic, because we won't be able to see cars coming round the bends – the high hedgerows block our view.'

Walking with dogs

- If you take your dog on a country walk, put it on a lead before you get out of the car.
- Keep the lead short so that the dog can't suddenly run into the road.
- Walk between the dog and the traffic, so that cars won't frighten it.

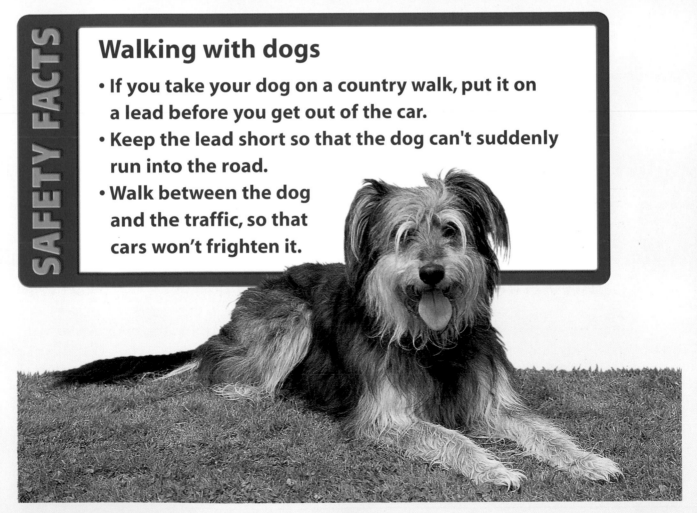

Crossing country roads

They walk further on and soon see some cows in a field. They look for a safe place to cross the road.

'This is no good,' says Mum, standing near a bend.

'Traffic coming towards us won't be able to see us.'

Railway lines

Sometimes, country roads cross a railway line. When a train is coming, lights flash, you hear an alarm and a stripy barrier comes down. Stop and wait until the train has passed before you cross the railway line.

A good crossing place

'Is this a better place?' asks Adam, when they reach a straight bit of road.
'Just fine,' says Mum. 'We can see clearly in both directions.'

They cross when the road is clear. The boys lean over a gate to look at a herd of cows.
'I think they are Friesians,' says Adam, with a grin.

'Thank you for bringing us here,' says Adam.
'I can't wait to tell my class where we've been.'

Glossary

Bollard Yellow and white marker on a traffic island in the middle of the road.

Bus lane Part of a road marked, usually in brown, for buses. It is sometimes used by taxis and cyclists too.

Cycle lane Part of a road or footpath reserved for use by cyclists.

Highway Code A booklet issued by the government, setting out the laws and rules for drivers, pedestrians, cyclists, motorcyclists and horse riders.

Junction The place where two roads meet.

Kerb The edge of a pavement.

Pavement A raised walkway at the side of a road where people can walk safely.

Pedestrian Any person who walks.

Pedestrian crossing A place where people can cross a road safely.

Pedestrian subway A pathway under a road.

Pelican crossing A pedestrian crossing with traffic lights controlled by the pedestrians.

Puffin crossing Pedestrian-friendly crossing with sensors controlling the traffic lights.

Reflective Something that sends light back from a surface, such as a car's headlights.

Safety barrier A metal fence running along part of a pavement that stops people from crossing that part of the road.

Traffic island A raised or marked place for pedestrians to stand in the middle of a road.

Traffic lights Red, amber and green lights which change in a particular order to tell traffic whether to stop or go.

Zebra crossing A pedestrian crossing with black and white stripes painted on the road and flashing Belisha beacons on poles.

Useful addresses and websites

BRAKE,
PO Box 548, Huddersfield, HD1 2XZ
www.brake.org.uk
Runs a road safety week with an action pack for schools.

Child Accident Prevention Trust,
18-20 Farringdon Lane, London EC1R 3HA
www.capt.org.uk
Provides downloadable factsheets on road safety, child road accidents and child pedestrians.

Department for Education and Skills (DfES),
PO Box 5050, Annesley, Nottingham NG15 0DJ
Produces A Safer Journey to School – a free guide on developing a school travel plan for parents and teachers.

Department for Transport (DfT)
Great Minster House, 76 Marsham Street,
London SW1P 4DR
www.thinkroadsafety.gov
A Department for Transport website for children aged 8-11
www.databases.dft.gov/uk/schools
A gateway to classroom materials encouraging greater use of walking, including walking buses and Safe Routes to Schools programmes.
www.roads.dft.gov.uk/roadsafety/child/index.htm
Lists available Department for Transport resources on child road safety.
www.local-transport.dft.gov.uk/schooltravel/index.htm
Provides a free School Travel Resource Pack.

Pedestrians Association,
126 Aldersgate Street, London EC1 4JQ
Produces a Walk to School information pack which encourages walking for school journeys, and Trail Blazers! – a guide to existing walking bus schemes.
www.pedestrians.org.uk

Royal Society for the Prevention of Accidents (RoSPA),
Edgbaston Park, 353 Bristol Road, Birmingham, B5 7ST
www.rospa.com
Provides both information and resources about the causes of road accidents.

Safety Street,
PO Box 2078, Reading, Berkshire RG30 3FF
www.safetystreet.org.uk
An interactive safety education centre which provides safety tours covering safety in the home, in the town, by canals, quarries and railways and on a building site, as well as on the road.

The Streetwise Safety Centre,
Unit 1 Roundways, Elliott Road, Bournemouth BH11 8JJ
www.streetwise.org.uk
An interactive safety education centre which provides safety tours covering safety in the home, in the town and on the beach, as well as on the road.

Sustrans,
35 King Street, Bristol BS1 4DZ
www.sustrans.org.uk and www.saferoutestoschools.org.uk
Sustrans co-ordinates the Safe Routes to School project, providing support for local authorities, schools and parents. It publishes newletters, teachers' packs, project guides and information sheets.

Young Transnet (YTN),
National Children's Bureau, 8 Wakely Street,
London EC1V 7QE
www.youngtransnet.org.uk
An interactive, child-centred website which encourages children to carry out surveys about school travel and enables them to compare results with other schools.

The Child Accident Prevention Foundation
www.kidsafe.com.au
A nationwide Australian charity providing lots of useful advice on the prevention of accidents.

Child Safety Foundation
www.childsafety.co.nz
A New Zealand website designed mainly for use by parents, which promotes all aspects of pre-school and early primary school safety.

Note to parents and teachers
Every effort has been made by the Publishers to ensure that these websites are suitable for children, that they are of the highest educational value, and that they contain no inappropriate or offensive material. However, because of the nature of the Internet, it is impossible to guarantee that the content of these sites will not be altered. We strongly advise that Internet access is supervised by a responsible adult.

Index